Maurice Pledger

Oscar Otter's STICKER BOOK

Written by A.J. Wood

By the River and Shore

templar publishing

A TEMPLAR BOOK

First published in the UK in 1999 by Templar Publishing,
an imprint of The Templar Company plc,
Pippbrook Mill, London Road, Dorking, Surrey, RH4 1JE, UK
www.templarco.co.uk

Illustration copyright © 1999 by Maurice Pledger/Bernard Thornton Agency, London
Text and design copyright © 1999 by The Templar Company plc

5 6 7 8 07 06

All rights reserved

ISBN-13: 978-1-84011-081-4
ISBN-10: 1-84011-081-3

Designed by Mike Jolley

Printed in Italy

How to use this book

On the following pages you'll find lots of sticker activities to do as you explore the river and shore with Oscar Otter and his animal friends.

You'll find animal Portrait Galleries to complete, outline sticker shapes to match, and you can also make up your very own pictures by adding stickers to the colourful scenes scattered throughout the book.

Just turn to the back of the book and you'll find all the stickers you need to have lots of fun. And when you've finished, you can reuse your stickers to make new pictures or to decorate your letters or notebooks.

Oscar Otter lives by the river. It is a wide, shining river that twists and turns through forests and fields until it finally reaches the sea.

Today, Oscar Otter is going to go exploring along the river bank. He hopes that he will meet some of his favourite animal friends along the way - Duggy the fluffy little duckling who lives on the pond, Hoppy the hopping frog and, if he makes it all the way to the seaside, he might even find his very best friend - Sidney the baby seal. Why don't you join Oscar on his great exploration and see how many new animal friends you can find on the way?

Oscar's friends

Oscar Otter has lots of animal friends. He hopes that he will meet some of them on his journey. His very best friend is Sidney Seal who lives at the very end of the shining river, at the edge of the great blue sea. You will meet him later in the book.

Use your stickers to fill in the Picture Gallery of some of Oscar Otter's friends. Which is your favourite animal friend?

Duggy Duckling   Hoppy Frog   Becky Beaver

Sophie Salmon   Sidney Seal   Sandy Seagull

Find five fish

Of all the creatures that live in Oscar's river, his favourite are the fish. Sometimes he eats them for his supper, but mostly he just likes to watch them swimming to and fro.

Once, Oscar found a goldfish swimming in his river. Now he is always on the look-out for new kinds of fish. Can you find five different ones for him to meet? Look on your sticker sheet and see if you can find five fishy friends to match the ones below.

Underwater friends

Fish are not the only creatures that Oscar finds when he goes exploring under the water. Use your stickers to fill in the Picture Gallery of five other underwater friends that Oscar has met.

Eel

Waterbeetle

Tadpole

Snails

Insect friends

It is a lovely sunny day when Oscar sets off on his journey down the river bank. He has not gone very far before he sees two colourful butterflies. What other insects do you think Oscar might meet by the river? Use your stickers to fill in the Picture Gallery of five other insect friends.

Dragonfly

Mayfly

Bumble Bee

Moth

Fly

13

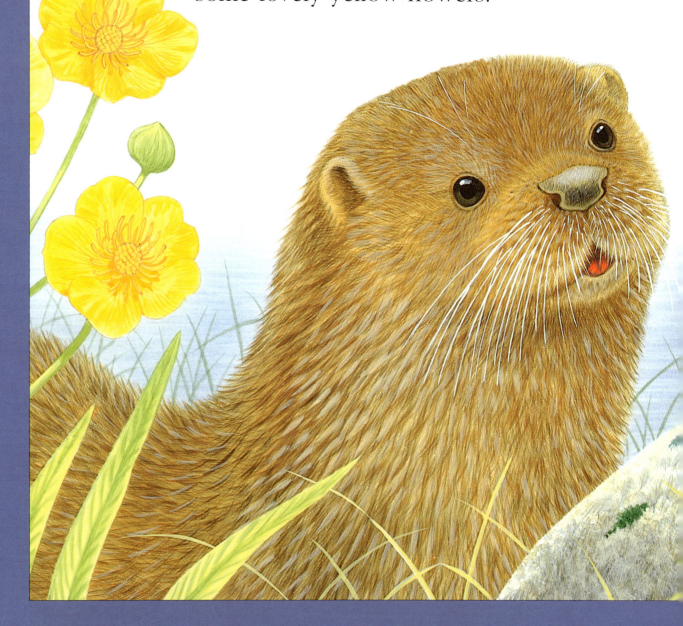

Who else do you think Oscar meets chasing insects down by the river? Why, it's Duggy Duckling and Hoppy Frog. Use your stickers to add them to this scene along with two dragonflies and some lovely yellow flowers.

Find five ducklings

Duggy Duckling likes to explore along the river too, but his favourite place to play is the old pond that the river runs through on its way to the sea. That's

because Duggy often meets lots of other ducklings there. There are Daisy and Dora, the yellow duckling twins, and Dippy, Duggy's very own brother. See if you can find them plus two other duckling stickers to match the ones below.

Use your stickers to make your very own picture of the pond where Duggy Duckling likes to play.

Whose baby?

I expect you know that a ***duckling*** is the name for a baby duck. But do you know that some other baby birds have special names, too? A baby goose is called a ***gosling***, and a baby swan is called a ***cygnet***. Use your stickers to put the right baby birds back with their parents. Which baby bird do you like best?

Feathered friends

Duggy has lots of other feathered friends that live by the river and pond. He loves to watch Katie Kingfisher flying over the water like a streak of blue lightning as she searches for fish. Use your stickers to fill in the Picture Gallery of Duggy's other bird buddies.

Here is Serena Swan, looking for Hoppy Frog. Can you help her by using your sticker to put him in the picture?

Add some colourful butterflies and two pretty water lilies to the scene as well.

Find five snails

Can you see what Hoppy Frog and Duggy Duckling have found by the old pond? Why, it's a stripy snail!

"Let's see how many other snails we can find," Hoppy suggests.

Why don't you help them by finding five snail stickers to match the ones below?

Frog friends

Hoppy isn't the only frog that lives on the old pond. Lots of his relatives live there, too. How many of them can you see in the picture? Now use your stickers to fill in the Picture Gallery of some of Hoppy's other pondside pals.

Nellie Newt

Terri Terrapin

Tommy Toad

Sammy Snake

Changing shape

Do you know that when Hoppy Frog was a baby he didn't look like a frog at all! Instead, he looked like a funny sort of fish, called a *tadpole*. Follow the numbers to see how a frog grows up.

6

Then use your sticker to put a fully grown frog in the space above.

1. A lady frog lays some eggs, called spawn, at the edge of the pond.
2. The eggs hatch into tiny tadpoles. They breathe through feathery gills on their heads.
3. As they grow they lose their feathery gills.
4. Gradually, their legs start to grow.
5. Soon they look like little frogs, but they still have their tadpole tail. As they get bigger, their tail gets shorter and shorter until...
6. Hey presto!

Bankside creepy crawlies

What creepy crawlies do you think Duggy Duckling is showing Oscar Otter on the river bank? He has found five different creatures.

"But no fish..." says Oscar.

"Time I carried on with my journey down the river!"

Slug

Beetle

Ladybird

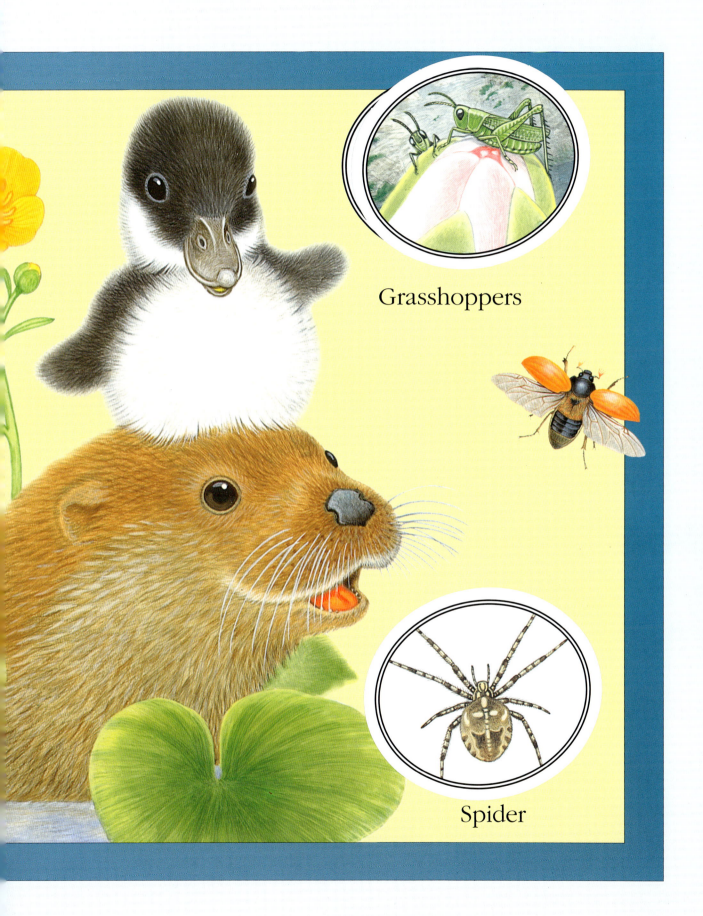

Grasshoppers

Spider

Look! Oscar has found a great pile of sticks in the middle of the river. Can you guess who they belong to? Why, it's Oscar's great friend Becky Beaver. Use your stickers to put her in the picture along with Swifty Swallow, a leaping fish and some colourful water lilies.

More furry friends

Becky Beaver isn't the only furry friend that Oscar meets on his journey to the sea. Lots of other animals visit the river from time to time. Bobby Bear comes to hunt in the shallows for a fish supper. Billy Bunny likes to chase butterflies up and down the bank.

Use your stickers to fill in the Picture Gallery of five furry friends that Oscar meets on his travels.

Who lives here?

Lots of animals build special homes on the river bank. Duggy Duckling lives in a feathery nest that his mother made amongst the reeds. Use your stickers to put the right animal back in its home and don't forget to add Duggy to the space below.

Becky Beaver makes a cosy home out of tree trunks and branches. It is called a *lodge*.

Katie Kingfisher makes her nest at the end of a long burrow, dug into the river bank.

Spiky Stickleback weaves a little ball of waterweed in which to lay her eggs.

Where is the sea, Sophie?

Oscar Otter is just wondering how much further it is to the sea when Sophie Salmon comes leaping along with her four salmon sisters.

"I've just come from the sea, it's that way!" she cries.

Use your stickers to put Sophie and her sisters in the picture.

It doesn't take long for Oscar to swim round the final bend in the river and there at last is the great blue ocean. Soon Oscar is sitting on a sandy beach looking for his best friend Sidney Seal.

Use your stickers to put Sidney in the picture opposite, along with a starfish, some seashells and some colourful seaweed.

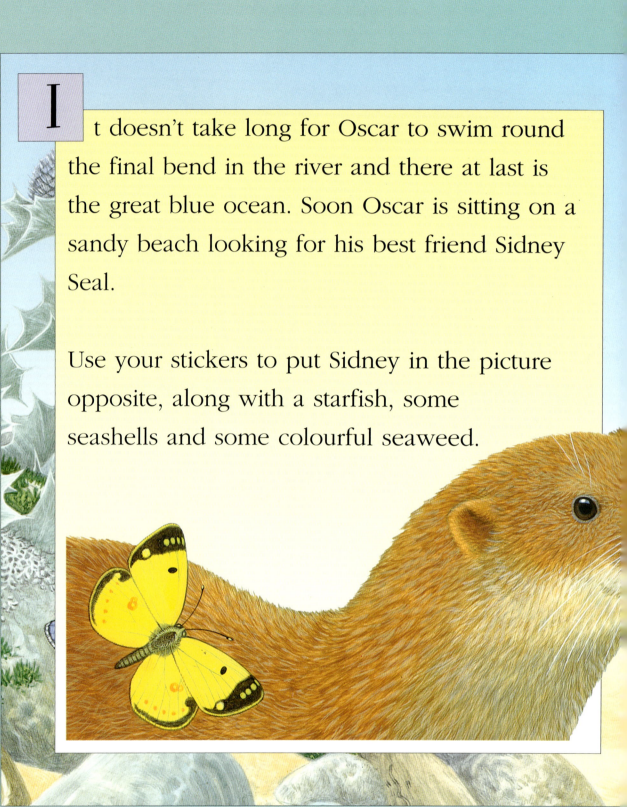

Find five starfish

Sidney has promised to help Oscar find some colourful fish, but first he wants to show him some other fascinating things that he has discovered on the seashore. Sidney's favourites are the starfish.

Can you find five different starfish for Oscar and Sidney to find?

Beach treasures

Sidney has a great collection of precious things that he has discovered on the beach. Sometimes he even finds real treasure! Use your stickers to fill in the pictures of his favourite finds!

Coral

Pebbles

Sea Urchin

Seaweed

Real Treasure - A ring!

Beachcombing

What other exciting things do you think Oscar and Sidney will find as they explore the beach? Make your own picture of some things that they might find washed up on the shore by adding

pebbles, shells,
a sea urchin, a
starfish and a crab to this picture.

Can you guess who Oscar and Sidney meet on their walk along the beach. Why, it's Sandy Seagull of course. Use your sticker to put her in the picture.

Now add a pretty flower, a beetle, some butterflies and a special kind of sea urchin called a sand dollar to the picture as well.

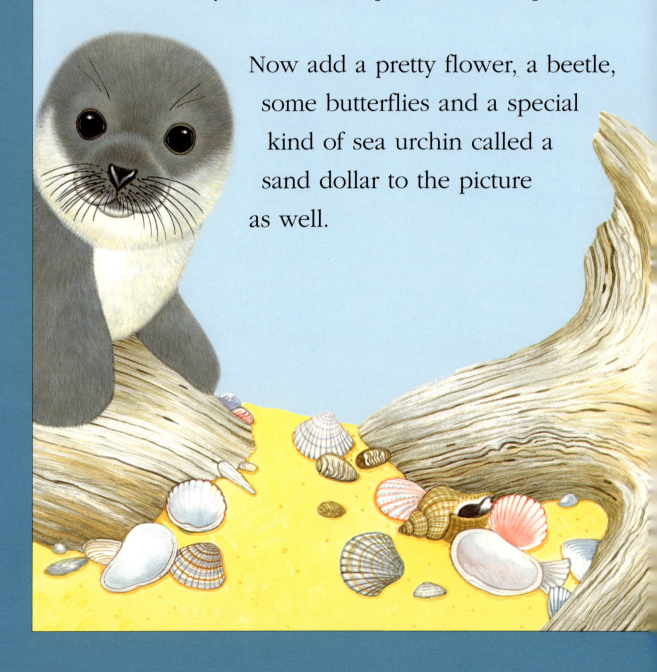

Find five crabs

Whenever Sandy Seagull goes exploring on the beach she always keeps her eye open for crabs. They come in all sorts of sizes and colours and she loves to watch them go scuttling sideways across the sand.
Can you find five different crab stickers to match the ones shown here?

Sandy's bird friends

Sandy Seagull isn't the only bird that Sidney Seal knows at the seaside. There are lots of other birds that come to hunt for food on the beach as well.

Use your stickers to fill in the Picture Gallery of four other birds that Sidney and Oscar might meet on their walk by the waves.

Gordon Gull   Olly Oystercatcher

Peter Plover   Tony Tern

Collecting shells

Do you ever collect shells when you're at the seaside? There are lots of different kinds, in all sorts of shapes and colours. See how many different ones you can find next time you're by the sea.

Now add lots of different shells to this beach scene.

Make up your own picture of the beach where Sidney Seal and Sandy Seagull live by adding stickers to this scene.

Rockpool friends

Oscar is very excited by all the things that he has seen on the beach, but he still really wants to find some fish. "I know!" says Sidney. "Let's go exploring in the rockpools. We're sure to find some fish there!" Use your stickers to fill in the Portrait Gallery of some of the creatures that they find.

Use your stickers to add some fish, a sea fan, a crab and a shrimp to this rockpool scene. Can you see what's hiding on the bottom?

An underwater story...

It's nearly time for Oscar to head back home. He is just about to say goodbye when Sidney's mum appears. She tells him all about the exciting things to be found far out at sea. Use your stickers to fill in the Picture Gallery of some of the things Oscar learns about from Sidney's mother.

And of course Sidney's mother has seen lots of fantastic fish on her underwater travels. Use your stickers to put them in the picture. Next time Oscar visits the beach he is going to go swimming with Sidney and his mum and see those fish for himself!

How to use your stickers

Look for the page numbers on the sticker sheets. They will help you find the right stickers for the different activities in this book.

Peel each sticker carefully from its backing sheet and stick it in the right place in the book. You can use the stickers again and again if you remember to treat them carefully.

Sheets 6 and 12 contain lots and lots of stickers for you to make up your own pictures. You can use them with the big scenes in the book. Or you could draw your own picture of the special place where Oscar Otter lives with all his animal friends and stick them on that!

Stickers for page 7

Sticker Sheet
1

Fish for page 9

Stickers for page 11

Stickers for page 11

Sticker Sheet 2

Stickers for page 13

Stickers for page 14

Stickers for page 17

Sticker Sheet
3

Stickers for page 20

Stickers for page 23

Stickers for page 22

Sticker Sheet 4

Snails for page 27

Stickers for page 24

Stickers for page 29

Stickers for page 32

Sticker Sheet

5

Frog for page 30

Stickers for page 34

Stickers for page 37

You'll find more furry friends
on sticker sheet 7

Stickers for page 18 - The Old Pond

Sticker Sheet 6

Stickers for page 40 - On the River Bank

Stickers for page 37

Sticker Sheet
7

Stickers for page 38

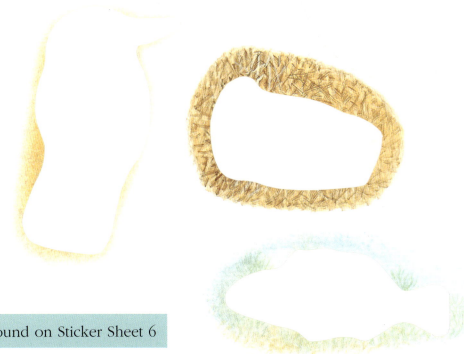

Stickers for page 40 can be found on Sticker Sheet 6

Salmon for page 42

Stickers for page 56

Sticker Sheet 10

Shells for page 59

Stickers for page 63

Stickers for page 60 can be found on Sticker Sheet 12